THE STORY OF

MALCOLM X,

CIVIL RIGHTS LEADER

THE STORY OF

MALCOLM X,

CIVIL RIGHTS LEADER

BY MEGAN STINE

A YEARLING BOOK

ABOUT THIS BOOK

The events described in this book are true. They have been carefully researched and excerpted from authentic autobiographies, writings, and commentaries. No part of this biography has been fictionalized.

To learn more about Malcolm X, ask your librarian to recommend other fine books you might read.

Published by
Dell Publishing
a division of
Bantam Doubleday Dell Publishing Group, Inc.
1540 Broadway
New York, New York 10036

Cover Photo Credit: UPI/Bettmann

Photographs on p. 55, *top*, p. 56, *top and bottom*, courtesy of Photographs and Prints Division, Schomburg Center for Research in Black Culture, The New York Public Library, Astor, Lenox and Tilden Foundations.

ISBN: 0-440-40900-4

Published by arrangement with Parachute Press, Inc.
Printed in the United States of America
January 1994
10 9 8 7 6 5 4 3 2 1
OPM

Contents

To Ruth and Jane

With gratitude for giving me the opportunity
to do such satisfying work

Author's Note

In reading and writing about Malcolm X, I have found that there are often different versions of the "truth" about many events in his life. Some of these differences are big, and some are small.

In his autobiography, for instance, Malcolm remembered some of the dates incorrectly—probably because the stories he was remembering had all happened so many years before. In other places Malcolm changed the names of people he knew, maybe to protect their privacy. Sometimes Malcolm told the stories from his childhood exactly as they were told to him—regardless of whether he actually thought they were true. Sometimes it is hard to know what is true and what is not—or to know what Malcolm really thought.

If you read *The Autobiography of Malcolm X,* as told to Alex Haley, you will find all these differences. You will also find differences between his book and the filmed version of Malcolm X's life by Spike Lee. And both of those versions are different from the way his life is told in other biographies, including this one.

But it is important to remember that there is probably a lot of truth in each portrait of Malcolm X. Each person who writes about Malcolm X has tried to bring

1

his or her own knowledge and understanding of him to light—to create a vision of this complicated, inspiring, and dynamic man.

In this book I have tried to present the most honest and complete portrait of Malcolm as I understand him. I have used his own words as inspiration, but I have also relied on the research done by other biographers. If you would like to learn more about Malcolm, you might want to start by reading *The Autobiography of Malcolm X* as told to Alex Haley. You might also want to read other books about him, some of which are listed below. Finally, you might want to read some of Malcolm's own speeches. His later speeches are collected in a book titled *Malcolm X Speaks,* edited by George Breitman.

Other books about Malcolm X:
Malcolm X as They Knew Him, by David Gallen
The Death and Life of Malcolm X, by Peter Goldman
Malcolm: The Life of a Man Who Changed Black America, by Bruce Perry
In Our Own Image: Critical Essays on Malcolm X, edited by Joe Wood

Born in Violence

"**F**ire! Wake up, Malcolm! Wake up!"

The shouts and screams came in the middle of a cool November night in 1929. Malcolm Little was snuggled in bed with his brothers and sisters. He was only four years old—too young to know what was happening, too young to remember very much. But he wasn't too young to understand that his house was on fire! It was a night he would never forget.

Amid the noise and commotion, Malcolm, his parents, and his brothers and sisters ran out of the burning house into their yard in rural Lansing, Michigan. The Littles were a big family. There were eight of them all together—Earl and Louise and their six children. Wilfred was Malcolm's oldest brother. Then came Hilda. Then Philbert, who at age six was just two years older than Malcolm. Reginald was two. And the baby of the family was Yvonne. She was born to Earl and Louise a few weeks before the fire.

Shivering in their underwear, the Littles watched their house burn down. Neighbors heard the noise, woke up, and came to help. But the fire department wouldn't come because they said the house was outside the city limits. Soon flames were leaping from the windows. No one could do anything to put out the fire. Within minutes the house was destroyed.

What had happened? Why was the house burning? And why did Malcolm's father shout "Let it burn!"?

Slowly two different stories emerged. Earl Little said the house had been set on fire by two white men—men who hated black people and wanted the Littles to leave the area. Earl said that he saw the white men running away and shot at them with his gun.

But the police told another story. They said that Malcolm's father had set the fire himself—for revenge.

Why would Earl want to burn down his own house?

There was only one possible reason: because it wasn't Earl's house anymore. Earl had bought the house in the summer of 1929. But after living there for just three months, he and his family were faced with an ugly surprise. The white man who sold Earl the house took him to court. He sued to get his house back. Amazingly, the court agreed he should get it. Why? Because Earl Little and his family were black!

The deed to Earl's property had a special clause in it. It said that the land could never be "rented, leased, sold to, or occupied by . . . persons other than those of the Caucasian race." In other words, black people weren't allowed to live there. Today that clause would be illegal. But in those days there were many laws, contracts, and property deeds that discriminated against black Americans.

In court the judge quickly took the property away from Earl Little and gave it back to the original owner.

The judge even ruled that the original owner didn't need to return the money Earl had paid him. He didn't have to give Earl a cent! To make matters worse, the judge ordered Earl to pay all the court costs and lawyers' fees. As a final blow, the judge gave the Littles no time to find a new home. He told them to leave immediately.

For the next two weeks Earl tried to stall. He asked his lawyer to appeal the court's decision. But everyone felt that he had no chance to win.

Then, that cold November night, the house went up in flames.

Had Earl set the fire himself to keep the original owner from taking the house back? That's what the police said. They even tried to arrest Earl for arson. But there wasn't enough evidence to make the charges stick.

Earl said that white racists had set the fire. He said those white people were trying to *force* the Littles to leave.

Many people believed Earl. They knew that black people were often the target of violence by whites. They also knew that sometimes the police helped to cover up white crimes against blacks. If white men burned down Earl's house, the police might ignore the crime—or look the other way.

Even now, no one knows for sure what happened that night.

All Malcolm knew was that his world had been set on fire. White people had come in the middle of the night. There had been shouts and violence. And the white neighbors stood around watching his house burn down. It was the earliest memory Malcolm X had—a memory that he later called a nightmare.

For a few weeks after the fire, Malcolm's family lived with friends. But a family of eight couldn't stay with friends for very long. Soon the Littles moved to a house in a white neighborhood in East Lansing. Immediately the violence started again. White neighbors threw stones at them. They made it clear they wanted the neighborhood's only black family to leave. Then Earl bought a farm in another all-white neighborhood.

Earl Little was trying to settle down. But it was hard for him to do that. He was an active person, always on the go. He had moved his family several times before and after Malcolm was born. Even when the family stayed put, Earl kept moving. He traveled all over the countryside in his work as a "visiting" Baptist preacher. Sometimes he preached in towns that were many miles away. Often he took young Malcolm with him.

When Earl wasn't preaching in church, he was preaching another kind of message. Malcolm's father was a member of a group called the Universal Negro Improvement Association, or UNIA. Led by a man named Marcus Garvey, UNIA believed that black people should be proud of their color and their heritage. Garvey said they should live separately from whites and should return to their homeland in Africa.

In the 1920s and 1930s, Garvey's beliefs were extremely unpopular with many white people. When Earl preached about Garvey's ideas, white people were shocked. Some whites told Earl that he should be like "the good Negroes" and go live in the black section of town.

But Earl paid no attention to them. He preached Garvey's message of African pride as often as he preached about Christian religion. He held small meetings with UNIA members at night, in different people's houses. And just as he had taken young Malcolm to church, he often took him to these meetings as well.

Malcolm was Earl's favorite child, and Malcolm knew it. Years later Malcolm remembered feeling special because he was the only child chosen to accompany his father. He liked going places with him. But it wasn't because he liked church or the UNIA meetings so much. He simply liked getting out of the house. At home, his mother and father fought a lot. Earl sometimes beat Malcolm's mother and whipped the other children. Since Malcolm was favored, though, Earl almost never punished him.

Although Earl didn't whip Malcolm, his mother did. Louise Little had been whipped often when she was young, so she brought up her children the same way. But whenever Malcolm's mother tried to punish him, he screamed so loudly that the neighbors could hear. Then his mother felt embarrassed and stopped beating him.

"I learned early that crying out in protest could accomplish things," Malcolm later said.

With screams and through favoritism, Malcolm managed to avoid most of his parents' abuse. But one day just after Malcolm had started school, he came home to find his parents fighting again. It was a fight Malcolm had heard them have before. They were arguing about what to have for dinner. Malcolm's parents often fought about food because his mother didn't believe in eating pork or rabbit. Although the family raised rabbits to sell to white people, Louise didn't want anyone in her own family to eat them. And that included Earl. But rabbit and pork were two of Earl's favorite foods.

This time the fight was worse than usual. Earl had gotten so mad that he went out into the yard and grabbed a rabbit. He killed the rabbit and threw it at her feet.

Crying, Malcolm's mother picked the rabbit up and started to clean it. She was going to cook it for her husband to put a stop to the fight. But Earl was so furious that he stormed out of the house and started walking toward town.

"Early! Early!" Louise called to him, using his full name. "If you go, you won't come back!" She ran after him into the road, calling to him and crying.

For a moment Earl turned around and waved to her. Then he kept on going.

All that night Louise cried. Somehow she sensed that Earl wouldn't come back. Many hours later, when the children were asleep, the police came to tell her that Earl had been found, almost dead, on some streetcar tracks. By the time Louise got to the hospital, Earl had died.

Malcolm and his brothers and sisters woke up when the police came and they heard Louise screaming and crying. But it wasn't until morning that they learned their father was dead.

Soon they began to hear the different stories about his death. Louise heard that the Black Legion had killed Earl. The Black Legion was a group of white racists much like the Ku Klux Klan. They dressed up in black robes instead of white sheets. Louise believed that the Black Legion had murdered Earl because of his work for UNIA. Then, according to her, they pushed his body onto the streetcar tracks to make the death look like an accident.

But the police told a different story. They said that Earl was still alive when they found him. One officer said that Earl explained the accident. He told the officer he had slipped and fallen while trying to board the streetcar. Earl said the streetcar driver couldn't see him in the dark.

Once again young Malcolm heard two different stories and didn't know which to believe. Were the police lying or were they telling the truth? Were they covering up for white racists again? Some people said one thing. Some people said another. It must have been hard for Malcolm to find the truth.

Falling Apart

After his father's death in 1931, Malcolm began to look to his older brothers for advice and protection. Wilfred, the oldest, quit school and went to work. But there were very few jobs available for adult black men in Lansing at that time. Only the most respected black men could expect to find steady work—as janitors or waiters or shoeshiners. Wilfred, who was only twelve years old, couldn't expect to get a "good" job like that. So he did odd jobs. The money he brought home was not nearly enough to feed their large family.

Malcolm's mother worked, too. She worked as a housekeeper or seamstress in the homes of white people in Lansing. But black people were not welcome— not even as housekeepers—in many white families' homes in Lansing. Often Louise was hired only because she had light skin and people thought she was white. When the families discovered that she was black, they fired her immediately. Then Louise moved on to another job—when she could find one.

With Wilfred and Louise gone most of the day, Malcolm was left to play with Philbert. As they grew up, Malcolm and Philbert fought constantly at home.

But at school they stuck together and fought the other boys, most of whom were white.

As time passed, Malcolm's family found it even harder to stay alive. Those were the Depression years, a time when there wasn't enough work, money, or food to go around. The Depression had started in 1929 and wouldn't be over for a few more years. Many families were hungry and poor, and Malcolm's was one of them. Some days Malcolm and Reginald walked two miles to a bakery in town and bought a big sack full of stale bread for a nickel. Then Louise would make bread pudding, or breadburgers, or stewed tomatoes and bread. She had about a dozen recipes for whole meals that were made out of little more than bread!

But sometimes they didn't even have a nickel to buy bread. Then Louise would go outside and pick dandelion greens. The neighbors teased them and said the family ate "fried grass."

Hunger began to eat away at Malcolm and his family. Sometimes they were so hungry, it made them dizzy. When things got this bad, Malcolm would eat whatever he could find. On the way to school he would pick wild leeks—a kind of onion—and make them into a sandwich.

Luckily for Malcolm, other classmates knew that he was hungry and tried to help. One girl brought extra food from home and shared her lunch with him. Other children invited him home for meals.

But Malcolm had to be careful when accepting charity. He knew that his mother had strict rules against it. For as long as she could, Louise refused to

11

take food from the state welfare agency. She was a proud woman, and she wanted her children to grow up with a sense of pride, too.

She also refused to accept food from friends—especially if the gift violated her dietary rules. One day the next-door neighbors offered her some pork. But Louise stubbornly turned it down. She was still just as strict about not eating rabbit, too, even when her children were starving. While Malcolm and his brothers could easily shoot wild rabbits, Louise wouldn't cook them. Instead, the children sold the rabbits to neighbors who bought them just to be kind.

But eventually the Littles were so hungry that Louise gave in. Two more children had been born into the family by now. (One child was Earl's son, Wesley. The other child, Robert, was born a few years after Earl died.) Now there were eight hungry children for Louise to feed.

So she began accepting help from the state welfare department. Then the welfare workers started coming to visit quite often. They made her "pay" for the food and her welfare check by letting them supervise how she raised her children. They told her that she was an unfit mother. Often the social workers took the children aside and asked questions about Louise.

With the social workers around, Louise changed, too. She resented their interference so much that she felt angry a lot of the time. She spent less time worrying about her children and didn't talk to them much.

In his autobiography, Malcolm said he felt as if his family's anchor were giving way. Slowly he began to drift off. He started hanging out around the stores in Lansing after school—and he began to steal. At first he just took apples and other treats because he was so hungry. Sometimes he got away with it. But other times he was caught.

Then the social workers came to his house again to criticize Louise. They said she wasn't raising Malcolm properly. They said she was "crazy" for refusing the neighbors' offer of pork. They began talking about taking Malcolm away from her and putting him in a foster home.

Years later, Malcolm blamed the welfare workers for tearing his family apart. He wrote in his autobiography that if they had just left his mother alone, everything would have been all right.

But they didn't leave Louise alone, and slowly but surely she became mentally ill. She talked to herself and sat around the house all day. She didn't cook or clean anymore. She began to think that people were trying to hurt her. She kept a knife handy, and sometimes she waved it around to threaten people, even friends.

Perhaps Louise would have had mental problems in any case. Or maybe Malcolm was right. Maybe the social workers wore her down and destroyed the family. Either way, it was a terrible thing for Malcolm and his brothers and sisters to see. They watched their mother deteriorate from a strong, strict, but loving woman into a woman who felt helpless, who had nowhere to turn.

Finally things were so bad at home that Malcolm and Philbert actually wanted to leave. They thought they would be better off in reform school! At least in reform school they would have enough food and a soft bed to sleep in at night. Together the brothers plotted a crime that would get them sent away from home. The next day they threw soft tomatoes at a passing motorist. But instead of calling the police, the driver simply whipped them and made them wash the car.

As the years went by, Malcolm's behavior became more of a problem. He continued to steal, defied his teachers, and broke the rules at school. Finally, at the age of thirteen, he was expelled from his neighborhood school and sent to live with a foster family. He was now in the seventh grade.

At first it seemed as if the move would do him some good. For one thing, he was now attending a school where, for the first time in his life, there were other black children in his class.

But Malcolm didn't mix with the black children at school any more than he mixed with the whites. He had few friends. He was a petty thief. His grades continued to drop.

Still, he didn't really seem to want to go back home, especially not now. When he did go home for a visit, it was painful for him. His mother was losing touch with reality and sliding into a severe state of mental illness. He couldn't stand to watch this happen to her.

In December of that year, 1938, Louise was found wandering around barefoot in the snow. She had her youngest child in her arms, and the baby was covered with sores. One month later the courts ordered Louise committed to the state mental hospital at Kalamazoo, Michigan. She lived there for the next twenty-six years.

Malcolm rarely saw his mother after that. Now with both parents gone, everything in his world had fallen apart.

Trying to Reform

After his mother was sent to the mental hospital, Malcolm decided to leave his foster home and go home to live with his brothers and sisters. Maybe things would be better now.

But Malcolm soon found that life at home hadn't really changed. The family was still poor. The social workers still came around all the time. Malcolm's older sister, Hilda, took care of the younger children. But she tried to mother them by being just as strict and demanding as Louise had been.

So within a few months of coming home, Malcolm asked the social workers if he could live in the county juvenile home instead. They agreed. They sent him to a place in nearby Mason, Michigan—a large building like a dormitory, with many private rooms. When Malcolm saw it, he was happy about one thing: here, for the first time in his life, he would have his own room.

The detention home was supervised by a white couple named Mr. and Mrs. Swerlein. The Swerleins lived there, ate meals with the children, and acted as their parents. Mrs. Swerlein was a big, strong woman who was strict but friendly to Malcolm. She liked him immediately, and he in turn went out of his way to please her. For a while Malcolm was almost happy.

At school Malcolm got top grades and was popular with his classmates. He was invited to join the debating team and the basketball team. He was even elected president of his eighth-grade class. During school assemblies, the teachers let Malcolm be responsible for keeping order in the balcony—and he did it well. He had a natural sense of authority and, at six feet tall, he commanded a lot of respect. It was easy for Malcolm to lead.

But no matter how popular Malcolm became, people were always ready to remind him that he was black. One teacher openly ridiculed him by saying that Africans had big feet—so big that "when they walk, they don't leave tracks, they leave a hole in the ground." The same teacher told "nigger" jokes and used the word *nigger* when Malcolm walked into class.

At sporting events Malcolm also heard the same ugly words quite a bit. When the basketball team traveled to other towns, the crowds would yell "Nigger!" and "Coon!" at him as he walked out onto the court. Even Mrs. Swerlein used the word *nigger* dozens of times a day, with Malcolm standing right next to her. Malcolm felt he was being treated like a pet or a mascot. To him it seemed as if the Swerleins thought they were his "owners." They clearly felt free to say whatever they pleased right in front of him, as if his feelings didn't matter—or as if he didn't understand.

But the worst moment for Malcolm came one day when he was alone with one of his favorite teachers, his English teacher, Richard Kaminska. Mr. Kaminska liked Malcolm and had usually praised his schoolwork. On this particular day, however, Kaminska wanted to talk about something else.

"Malcolm," Kaminska said. "You ought to be thinking about a career. Have you given it any thought?"

Kaminska was known around the school for always urging his students to work hard to achieve their goals, so Malcolm wasn't surprised when the topic came up.

"Well, yes, sir," Malcolm replied. "I've been thinking I'd like to be a lawyer."

Mr. Kaminska looked surprised. Instead of encouraging Malcolm, he said nothing for a minute. He leaned back in his chair. Then he told Malcolm that his goal wasn't realistic.

"Don't misunderstand me, now. We all like you here, you know that. But you've got to be realistic about being a nigger," Mr. Kaminska said. He went on to suggest that Malcolm should consider being something he *could* be—like a carpenter, for instance.

Malcolm was crushed. He knew that Mr. Kaminska did not tell his white students to be "realistic." On the contrary, he always encouraged them to strive for greater success—even though the other students' grades were not as good as Malcolm's.

From that moment on, as Malcolm later said in his autobiography, he started to change inside. He began to resent the word *nigger,* even though he had previously been able to ignore it. Now he felt angry with white people, and he let it show. He wasn't as friendly or cooperative with his teachers as he had been before. Pretty soon everyone began asking him what was wrong.

But Malcolm didn't tell them. He had always been a private person—and now he was more so. From then on, he kept his feelings inside.

The conversation with Mr. Kaminska was the first of two important events that changed young Malcolm's life. The second event was the arrival of a visitor from Boston—a visitor named Ella.

Ella was Malcolm's half-sister, Earl Little's daughter from his first marriage. Ella was a big, proud woman who looked and acted as if she knew what she wanted—and could get it. Ella seemed proud of her blackness and proud of her family ties, too. Even though Malcolm had never met her before, he liked her right away.

From the moment she arrived, Ella took charge of everything and told everyone what to do. Then she drove all the Little children to visit Louise in the mental hospital. The trip must have made them feel like a family again—at least for that one day.

Before Ella left, she invited Malcolm to come visit her in Boston. So the next summer, when school was out, Malcolm went.

The visit to Ella's became a major turning point in Malcolm's life. After seeing Boston, he would never think of Michigan—or himself—in the same way.

Young Hipster

Malcolm's trip to Boston in 1940 was a series of firsts. It was his first visit to a big city filled with bright lights, exciting nightclubs, swinging music, and wonderful restaurants. It was the first time Malcolm ever saw sophisticated, wealthy black people. He was amazed by the fine clothes he saw and the upper-class accents he heard among Boston's socially prominent blacks. And it was the first time he was treated as if he had a lot of potential—as if his future mattered.

But what Malcolm remembered most was that this was simply the first time he had ever been surrounded by so *many* other black people. Being among black people made Malcolm feel comfortable with himself as a black American. It was a feeling he didn't want to give up.

When he got back to Michigan after the visit, Malcolm felt restless and dissatisfied. He was no longer happy with the small-town life of Mason. It just didn't compare with the excitement of Boston. And he was no longer willing to be treated the way Mrs. Swerlein treated him—as if he were a "nice nigger." In 1941, less than a year later, Malcolm wrote to Ella and begged her to let him come live with her permanently.

Ella said yes, and soon the courts gave her legal custody of Malcolm. By the time he was fifteen years old, he had left Michigan for good.

Life in Boston was a complete change for Malcolm for several reasons. Although Ella lived in a poor black neighborhood in Boston, Roxbury, she lived in the fanciest part—a section called the Hill. The people who lived on the Hill thought they were better than the other residents of Roxbury. Ella owned her own house there, and she also owned a country house. There was always plenty to eat at Ella's and nice clothes to wear.

Also, Ella didn't expect Malcolm to go to school. She *did* expect him to get a job eventually, but even that could wait. She told him to take some time to see Boston first.

So Malcolm explored the city. He found two areas that attracted him most. One was the ghetto of Roxbury—the neighborhood that wasn't fancy like the Hill. The ghetto had pool halls and pawnshops and bars. Malcolm was drawn to the action in a way he couldn't resist.

The other place was the Roseland State Ballroom. The most famous big bands of the era played music there each night, and Malcolm was dazzled. Back in Michigan, he and his schoolmates had only been able to listen to bands such as Count Basie and Glenn Miller on records. Now Malcolm was living in a city where he could actually go see those musicians in person! Of course, Malcolm would have to wait for the night when the bands played for black customers, because dances held at the Roseland Ballroom were segregated. Most of them were for whites only, but sometimes there would be a dance held for blacks.

Soon Malcolm struck up a friendship with a man who worked in a poolroom in the ghetto. In his autobiography Malcolm called him Shorty. But Shorty wasn't his real name. It was a fictional name used to represent a number of Malcolm's friends, including his close friend Malcolm Jarvis. Since Malcolm was over six feet tall, most of his friends were "Shorty" to him.

Shorty taught Malcolm all about the street life at the time. He taught him to speak "hipster" slang, using such words as *daddy-o, cat, chick,* and *cool.* He pointed out the hustlers in the neighborhood who made money from selling drugs, stealing, gambling, and other illegal activities. But Shorty also helped Malcolm get his first real job—shining shoes at the Roseland Ballroom!

Malcolm thought he was in heaven. Working at the Roseland was like a dream come true. Every night he brushed elbows with the famous musicians he so admired. Every night he heard great music—and got to watch great dancers doing the lindy-hop on the ballroom floor.

And every night Malcolm made money from more than just shining shoes. Freddie, who taught Malcolm his job shining shoes, also taught him how to "hustle" the customers. Some of the hustles were not against the law. For instance, since the shoeshine stand was in the men's restroom, Malcolm could offer towels to the customers after they washed their hands. That earned him a nickel tip. He could also earn a tip for brushing lint off a customer's suit. Or he could sell shoelaces.

But soon Malcolm learned that there were other ways to hustle customers. He sold marijuana cigarettes, called reefers, to the musicians who traveled in the bands. He also sold liquor illegally to many of the men who came to dance. Hustling earned Malcolm a lot more money than shining shoes.

Ella didn't approve of Malcolm's job at the Roseland. She thought a shoeshine job wasn't good enough for him. But she couldn't make him quit. After a while, he was making enough to buy a sky-blue zoot suit, and the store let him pay for it a little at a time. A zoot suit was a wild outfit. The jacket had huge padded shoulders, a tiny waist, and long, tuxedo-like coattails. And the pants were enormously baggy at the knees. Then they tapered down so they were tight around the ankles.

Ella was horrified. But try as she might to run Malcolm's life, she knew she couldn't do it. He was sixteen years old now and looked much older. Most of the people he hung around with were grown men. His friends thought he was in his twenties.

The zoot suit was more than a cool outfit to Malcolm. It was a way of telling the world that he was part of a certain crowd. The young black men who wore zoot suits in 1942 were trying to set themselves apart from mainstream society. Their zoot suit was a symbol of their resistance and independence as they struggled to be recognized as full citizens in this country. They weren't willing to go off to Europe to fight World War II. But they also weren't willing to be treated as if they were "boys." Wearing a zoot suit was an act of rebellion and pride on Malcolm's part—his first step in growing toward manhood.

To go with the zoot suit, Malcolm got a matching sky-blue hat with a feather in it. And then he let a friend talk him into one more thing that was in fashion. He conked his hair.

Conking was a hair-straightening process that many black men used in those days. Malcolm couldn't wait to conk his hair, but he had no idea how much it would hurt. His friend Shorty told him what to buy at the drugstore. Then Shorty mixed the ingredients for the conk and poured them onto Malcolm's head. Within a few minutes Malcolm's head was burning so much he thought it was on fire. He ran to the sink and begged Shorty to wash out the burning chemicals as fast as he could.

Despite the pain involved, Malcolm loved his conk so much that he continued to straighten his hair the same way for the next several years. The process also turned his reddish hair an even brighter red. People began using Malcolm's hair color as his nickname.

Everyone called him Red.

Malcolm yearned to spend more time at the Roseland—but not in the men's room. With his zoot suit and conked hair, he wanted to be out having fun, dancing the lindy-hop on the ballroom floor. So he quit his shoeshine job and became a regular at the black dances. Sometimes he would compete in the dance contests, dancing with certain black girls who were well known for their style on the Roseland floor. A few times he took a girl named Laura to the Roseland. She was a respectable girl he had met on the Hill.

But one night a new woman caught his eye. She was blond and older than Malcolm—one of several white women who occasionally hung out at the black dances. Malcolm said these women came for the excitement of mixing with a black crowd. In his autobiography he called this woman Sophia.

Soon Malcolm and Sophia were a pair. They were seen around town together, especially in his neighborhood. But Ella didn't care for this friendship. Quickly she came up with a scheme to get Malcolm out of town. She got him a job on the railroad.

Malcolm was happy to take the job Ella had lined up because it got him a free ride to New York City—a place he had always wanted to see. Besides, riding the trains from Boston to New York wasn't so bad. Malcolm made sandwiches and sold them to the passengers. And being on the train kept him moving. Malcolm was always happiest when he was on the go.

But Malcolm was not about to give up Sophia. He continued to see her every time he was back in Boston—which turned out to be several times a week! Eventually he quit his railroad job and stayed in New York. But Sophia was still in the picture. Over the years she supplied Malcolm with clothes, money, and an apartment.

When Malcolm got to Harlem, he was once again a newcomer in a big city. He was awed by this uptown section of New York City, with its nightclubs and sophisticated people. In the daytime he saw well-dressed black men who wore conservative business suits, not zoot suits. They sat around and talked quietly in a restaurant and nightclub called Small's Paradise. Malcolm was impressed by their behavior. It seemed dignified, and therefore more attractive, than the way many of his friends behaved.

At night Malcolm saw that Harlem was filled with white people who came uptown to hear the music and feel the excitement of Harlem's famous nightlife. Once Malcolm had tasted the glamour of Harlem, Boston held little appeal.

With luck, Malcolm soon managed to land a job in the one place he liked best: Small's Paradise. Charlie Small had just a few simple rules for his employees. No lateness, no laziness, no stealing—and most of all, no one was allowed to hustle the customers.

For a while Malcolm waited on tables and tried to follow the rules, but one day he hustled a customer. When Charlie Small found out, he fired Malcolm.

After that, Malcolm was back out on the streets. And the streets of Harlem were tough. Soon Malcolm was selling marijuana to musicians—and using drugs himself. Then for a while he was a numbers runner—he passed along bets for illegal gambling. Later, other hustles came along. He even robbed neighborhood stores.

Every now and then Malcolm would get a regular job in New York or Boston. But those jobs never lasted long.

As he said years later, he was the lowest of the low. Malcolm wrote in his autobiography, "I had sunk to the very bottom of the American white man's society."

And when he looked back on his life of crime, Malcolm wasn't proud of what he had become.

He was proud of one thing he accomplished during those years, though. He managed to stay alive during World War II—by staying out of the army. Malcolm believed that it was foolish for black men to fight for white America when white Americans cared so little about the rights of black people.

So when it was time for Malcolm to report to the draft board, he told everyone he wanted to join the *Japanese* army. He went to the draft board dressed in his zoot suit and acting crazy. He told the army psychiatrist that he *wanted* to join the army and hoped to be sent down south. Then, he said, he would organize other black soldiers in the South to "steal us some guns, and kill up crackers!"

Malcolm's wild act worked. The draft board classified him as 4-F, which meant he was unfit for service.

Finally, in 1945, Malcolm returned to Boston and to Sophia, who was married now. With her help Malcolm and a few friends began doing something they had never done before. They began burglarizing private homes.

The system was easy. Sophia and two of her girlfriends knew many of the wealthiest people in Boston. So they would select houses for Malcolm and his friend Malcolm Jarvis to burglarize. Sometimes Sophia and her friends would actually "case the joint" ahead of time. Other times the women simply pointed out which families were out of town.

The burglaries went on for several weeks. Then one day Malcolm made a big mistake. He took a stolen watch with a broken crystal to a pawnshop to have it repaired. The watch was very expensive, and Malcolm was planning to keep it for himself.

But the pawnshop owner recognized the watch as stolen property and called the police. When Malcolm came back a few days later to pick up the watch, he was arrested.

At the police station Malcolm confessed to his crimes. He also cooperated by giving the police the names of his accomplices—including Sophia. In return, he was promised that the judge would give him a lighter sentence.

A month later, in February 1946, Malcolm and his friends went on trial. Malcolm pleaded guilty, and eventually so did one of the other two men. Sophia, on the other hand, testified that the men had forced her to help out with the crimes.

The women were ultimately sentenced to one to five years in jail.

But the men were punished much more severely for their crimes. Malcolm got ten years of hard labor. Malcolm Jarvis was sentenced to eight to ten years. The usual sentence for a first offender was about two years in jail.

During the trial Malcolm commented to his lawyer that he seemed to be on trial for more than just burglary.

"We seem to be getting sentenced because of those girls," Malcolm said. He meant because the women were white and the men were black.

"You had no business with white girls!" his own lawyer shot back.

Prison

In February 1946, at the age of twenty, Malcolm went to prison. The prison he was sent to, in Charlestown, Massachusetts, was only a few miles from where he had lived in Boston. But living in prison was very different from his former way of life.

Charlestown Prison itself was almost 150 years old. It had been built in 1805 and had never been modernized.

Malcolm's cell was dirty and small—about eight feet long and six feet wide. Lying on his cot, he could easily touch the opposite wall. There were rats and lice in the cells. Instead of a toilet, each cell had only a covered bucket. The smell from the bucket never went away.

When Malcolm first arrived there, he was put into solitary confinement for one day, just to let him know what it was like. The regular cell was bad enough. But in solitary there were no windows and no bed. The cell was pitch-black.

After his day in solitary, Malcolm was allowed to have visitors. Soon Ella came to see him. But Malcolm and Ella had very little to say to each other. Malcolm was probably still angry with Ella because she hadn't helped him more during his trial. He knew that she had enough money to get him a good lawyer, but she hadn't done it.

For her part, Ella probably felt bad about not helping Malcolm. Years later she admitted that she had wanted him to go to prison. She thought a year or two in jail might straighten him out. But when Malcolm was sentenced to ten years of hard labor, Ella cried out in the courtroom. She knew she had made a terrible mistake.

After that first visit, Ella tried to help by sending money. But Malcolm used the cash to buy marijuana and other drugs, which he bought from the guards! The guards sold drugs to the prisoners to make a little extra money on the side. Like many of the other inmates, Malcolm stayed "high" in prison almost as much as he had when he was out.

All in all, his first year in Charlestown was miserable. Malcolm must have felt angry much of the time, and he showed it by cursing nonstop. Since much of his ranting and swearing was against the Bible, God, and religion, the other prisoners came up with a nickname for him. They called him Satan. But Malcolm didn't appear to mind. It made him seem like a tough guy.

Then one day Malcolm met an inmate who was a prison leader even though he didn't act tough. The man's name was John Elton Bembry. Like Malcolm, Bembry was a convicted burglar, but much older and more mature. He'd been in prisons for many years. Bembry was extremely smart and very well read. He had read all kinds of literature, including books by

Shakespeare, Melville, and Thoreau. He had also read dozens of books about philosophy, history, and religion. He was the prison library's most frequent visitor.

Everyone in Charlestown Prison respected Bembry as an intellectual leader. Prisoners and guards alike would sit around after their day's work was done, listening to him talk on any subject that came into his mind. On many occasions the subject was religion. Malcolm listened from the sidelines and was impressed by how much Bembry knew.

"He was the first man I had ever seen command total respect with his *words*," Malcolm later noted in his autobiography.

But try as he might, Malcolm couldn't figure out how to make friends with Bembry. Bembry seemed gruff and unapproachable except when he was speaking to a group. He almost never spoke to Malcolm. He didn't seem to welcome private conversations or even want to make friends.

So one day, when all the prisoners were in the courtyard, Malcolm walked past the bench where Bembry was playing dominoes. He "accidentally" knocked over Bembry's dominoes, then kept walking in a circle around the yard. A few minutes later he stopped in front of the bench again. Bembry stood up. At first Malcolm just stared at him. Bembry thought he was trying to start a fight. Then Malcolm finally spoke.

Malcolm's first questions to Bembry were about religion. Bembry answered Malcolm by talking to him about ideas rather than feelings. Malcolm was impressed with Bembry's answers—and by the fact that Bembry never used a foul word. Over time, Malcolm and Bembry became friends.

Then one day Bembry told Malcolm that he "had some brains"—and he should use them. At first Malcolm was annoyed at being told what to do. But he admired Bembry too much to curse at him or argue with him. And besides—Malcolm *was* very smart. He had a deep hunger for knowledge that he had not even begun to satisfy. Soon he began to take Bembry's advice. He began to educate himself.

First Malcolm took some courses by mail, studying English and Latin. Then he began to read. He read everything in the prison library that interested him and many books that Bembry recommended, too.

When he first began to read, Malcolm particularly liked Aesop's fables. He could really relate to the fox in the stories, who was always trying to outwit the other animals! In fact, years later one of Malcolm's friends said that the best way to understand Malcolm was to picture him as a fox.

But eventually Malcolm moved on to more challenging reading. He tried reading the Greek philosophers, such as Plato and Socrates. He wanted to read volumes of world history. He even tackled Shakespeare. But he soon found that he had trouble understanding many of these books because his vocabulary wasn't strong.

So Malcolm set out to improve his vocabulary by reading and writing every single word and definition in the dictionary. Then he went back to the classic books and read them again. He read the Greek philosophers, and this time he understood them very well. By the time he was released from prison, six years later, he had read far more than most college graduates. He had changed himself from a petty criminal into a serious, self-taught man of learning. Now he was so well educated that he was able to discuss almost any topic with a great deal of understanding and depth.

Finding Allah

For almost a full year Malcolm endured the horrible conditions at Charlestown Prison. Then in January 1947 he was transferred to a different prison, the Concord Reformatory. Life was easier there than it had been at Charlestown. The inmates had toilets instead of buckets in their cells. And they had more chances to mix socially. This reformatory actually had a dining hall, which meant that the prisoners were allowed to leave their cells for meals. That was a big change from Charlestown, where Malcolm had eaten every meal alone.

But Malcolm wasn't exactly happy. What he really wanted—what he was working toward—was yet another transfer. He desperately wanted to be sent to the prison colony at Norfolk, Massachusetts. At Norfolk the prisoners had comfortable rooms. And they were given many more privileges than in standard prisons.

Every so often Malcolm sent letters to the authorities, asking for a transfer to Norfolk. At the same time, Ella was sending similar requests.

But while Malcolm was waiting and hoping for word from the top, he got a letter of a different kind.

His brother Philbert wrote to tell him that he had discovered the "natural religion for the black man." Philbert didn't give Malcolm many details, except to say that the group was called the Nation of Islam. Philbert and three of Malcolm's other brothers and sisters—Wilfred, Hilda, and Reginald—had all joined this group. Philbert told Malcolm to pray to Allah for "deliverance."

Malcolm read the letter and laughed at it. His brother Philbert had been involved in many religions through the years. Philbert was always writing to Malcolm and saying that he would pray for him. So Malcolm thought this was just one more of Philbert's religious fads. Malcolm still didn't believe in God. And he still didn't have much respect for anyone who was caught up in a religious cause. In fact, he wrote back an angry reply to Philbert, saying he wasn't at all interested.

A short time later another letter came for Malcolm. This one was from his younger brother Reginald. Instead of talking about religion, Reginald just gave Malcolm little bits of news from home. Then he wrote: "Don't eat any more pork, and don't smoke any more cigarettes. I'll show you how to get out of prison."

Now Malcolm was interested. He started thinking about Reginald's letter day and night. Had Reginald come up with some kind of hustle that would get him out of prison? Malcolm thought there must be some trick or scam that Reginald was trying to pull to help him get out—and that it involved not eating pork or smoking cigarettes.

Without even knowing why he was doing it, Malcolm decided to take Reginald's advice. He gave up cigarettes almost immediately—and never smoked another one as long as he lived. The next time pork was served in the dining hall, Malcolm passed the platter along without taking any. When the man next to him looked surprised, Malcolm simply said, "I don't eat pork."

Almost immediately word got around. Everyone in the prison was talking about Malcolm. The white prisoners were especially surprised that Malcolm would give up pork. They thought that black people liked pork too much to give it up. Malcolm felt proud knowing that he had done something other people considered hard.

Sometimes, passing up pork meant Malcolm went hungry. Pork was served a lot in prison. But Malcolm didn't mind. All he wanted was to find out why he was doing this. What was the trick his brother had planned?

Malcolm wasn't a very patient person, so it was hard for him to wait. And he didn't get an answer right away. But a few months later, toward the end of 1948, a different wish came true. Malcolm was finally transferred to Norfolk!

Norfolk was almost paradise compared with the other two prisons. Malcolm had his own room, with a door instead of bars. There were showers and toilets, and the building was clean. There were also many activities—Ping-Pong, sports, gardening, debates, classes, and group discussions. Malcolm, like the other prisoners, was free to wander around inside the building. Visitors could come almost every day.

But the best thing about Norfolk, as far as Malcolm was concerned, was the library. It was enormous, containing thousands of books. There were more books than would fit on the library shelves. A millionaire named Lewis Parkhurst had left the books to the prison in his will. Many of them were about history and religion. Those were the two topics that had interested Parkhurst, and interested Malcolm, the most.

One day, though, Malcolm's reading was interrupted by a visitor. Reginald had finally come—and Malcolm was hoping that he had come to explain at last about not eating pork.

But Reginald took his time getting to the point. Instead he talked about other things—such as news from home—for quite a while. Then, when Malcolm was about to burst with curiosity, Reginald began to talk about religion.

Slowly Reginald explained the beliefs of the Nation of Islam. But he didn't just pour out all the information at once. He told it to Malcolm like a puzzle or a riddle . . . unfolding each part when he sensed that Malcolm was ready to listen.

The Nation of Islam, as Reginald explained, was led by a black man named Elijah Muhammad. Muhammad was called the Messenger because he was believed to be God's messenger here in America. According to Reginald, God's real name was Allah—and Allah was a man. Reginald also said that the devil was a man.

Malcolm was intrigued. He wanted to know who this devil was. Reginald nodded toward some white people on the other side of the room. "Them. The white man is the devil," Reginald said.

Malcolm was stunned. For years he had wanted to be accepted by white people. But when he thought about all the white people he had known, he realized that very few of them had been truly kind to him. Very few had shown any respect for him. He asked Reginald if there could be any exceptions. Were *all* white people devils?

Reginald said that even the white people who seemed sympathetic to blacks were devils. They were actually using black people and taking advantage of them.

Reginald went on to show Malcolm how white people had taken away all the black people's pride. He pointed out that black history was never taught in schools. He reminded Malcolm that black Americans had originally come from Africa—but that none of them knew their original African family names.

"You wouldn't recognize your true language if you heard it," Reginald said.

He also told Malcolm that the history of the African people was a story of a great civilization and great accomplishments. But now whites were taking credit for all the things black people had done.

As Reginald's words began to sink in, Malcolm felt as if he were in a state of shock. It was almost as if he had been hit by lightning. He hardly ate anything or spoke to anyone for days. He didn't quite know what to think about Reginald's ideas. But somehow he was opening his mind to them.

A few days later Reginald visited again. He went on to explain the basics of the religion. The Nation of Islam practiced a form of the religion called Islam. Like all believers in Islam, members of the Nation were called Muslims. And in many ways the members of the Nation were like the millions of Muslims in the Middle East. They worshipped Allah and prayed toward the holy city of Mecca several times each day. They followed the Muslim rules about cleanliness, including washing their hands and faces before praying. Like all Muslims, they did not eat pork.

But—although Reginald did not say this to Malcolm at the time—the Nation of Islam was different from traditional Islam. The Nation had some different rules and beliefs, rules that came from their leader, Elijah Muhammad. These beliefs set them apart from the rest of the Muslims in the world. For instance, traditional Muslims do not believe that all white people are devils. In fact, in places like Bosnia, a country in Eastern Europe, many blond-haired, blue-eyed people are Muslims. And traditional Muslims do not have the same strict rules of behavior that the Nation had.

In the Nation of Islam, Elijah forbade his followers to smoke, drink liquor, dance, gamble, or use any drugs. There were rules about how unmarried men and women could behave together. And no one was allowed to say anything against Elijah Muhammad. If a follower broke these rules, he or she could be thrown out of the temple and ignored by all the other Muslim members.

The rules may have seemed harsh, but the Nation of Islam attracted many followers—partly because many people enjoyed the sense of pride that came from following a strict, disciplined lifestyle. Elijah's followers were also willing to make personal sacrifices because they believed in the message he was promoting—a message of black strength, unity, and pride.

Another difference between the Nation of Islam and traditional Muslims was what they called their houses of worship. In the Nation, they called them temples. But all other Muslims call their houses of worship mosques. Years later, when the Nation learned the correct term, they renamed their temples and began calling them mosques.

The biggest difference between the Nation of Islam and other Muslims, however, had to do with the history of the world that was taught by Elijah Muhammad.

According to Elijah, the first thing that happened was that the moon was blasted out of the center of the earth. After that, he said, the first people on earth were black. For many years these black people had a rich and intelligent civilization. But one of these early men was a genius scientist named Yacub. Yacub was so smart that he had a very large head. According to the story of Yacub, he was a troublemaker. So he and 59,999 of his followers were sent away to an island to live.

There Yacub decided to create a devil race of

bleached-out white people. So he formed a plan. He believed that all black people had two "germs"—one for black skin and one for brown. Yacub declared that only brown babies would be allowed to live. Then, over time, as each generation produced lighter- and lighter-skinned babies, Yacub's plan would finally succeed. Eventually he would produce a race of weak, evil, white devils.

According to this story, it took eight hundred years to produce the white devil race. The story went on to say that the white devil race was expected to rule the world for six thousand years. But finally a time would come when Allah would destroy the white race and black people would once again return to their rightful places as rulers on earth. As a signal that this time was coming, a black man would appear who had great wisdom and knowledge. This man would be Allah's messenger.

Elijah Muhammad said *he* was the Messenger—and the Nation of Islam's members believed him.

Malcolm learned all of this over the next few months from letters sent to him by his brothers and sisters. His sister Hilda also visited and urged him to accept the teachings of the Nation of Islam.

At first Malcolm felt confused and unsure. But in a relatively short time he began to believe what his brothers and sisters said.

Finally he wrote a letter to Elijah Muhammad. Malcolm wanted his letter to be well written, so he copied it over dozens of times. When an answer came back from the Messenger himself, Malcolm felt "electrified." Somehow the Nation of Islam had more reality now. Malcolm also appreciated the five-dollar bill that Elijah enclosed in the envelope.

It took a number of months before Malcolm felt truly converted to Islam. First he had to make himself kneel down to pray. Malcolm had a very hard time doing that. He knew it was a sign of submission to Allah, and he did not want to submit himself to anyone.

But when Malcolm finally did succeed in bending his knees for prayer, then he felt he truly understood Islam. After all, Malcolm thought, *Islam* is an Arabic word that means "submission."

From that moment on it was as if the old, hustling Malcolm had vanished. Now there was only Malcolm the true believer. The new Malcolm gladly gave up everything for his belief in Allah. This religion seemed to fill a deep need he had—the need to believe in his own people and to take pride in himself.

To show the depth of his belief, Malcolm shaved his head. He stopped using slang and started reading more and more about history and religion. He also began a letter-writing campaign. He wrote to all the drug pushers, gamblers, and other criminals he had known, telling them about the Nation of Islam and Elijah Muhammad. Not surprisingly, Malcolm didn't manage to convert them by mail. In fact, none of them ever answered his letters.

But he did manage to convert some of the black inmates at the Norfolk penal colony. He told them that the white man had "whitewashed" history and deprived them of the truth about their past. He told them about the history of slavery. He told them that the white man was the devil.

Some inmates were not open to Malcolm's ideas, but many were. Within a year he had found at least a dozen followers.

At the same time, Malcolm joined the prison's debate team. Soon he learned to be a powerful public speaker. Debate teams from Harvard and Yale came to the prison, and Malcolm eagerly prepared to confront them. Sometimes he won the debate by quoting British history. Sometimes he won by pointing out the racial issues the topic raised. But no matter what his strategy, it gave him an exhilarating, powerful feeling to be able to persuade an audience and control his opponents that way.

He also studied politics and law and learned how to use this knowledge to get what he wanted from the prison officials. For example, at one point he and a few other Muslims requested cells facing east so they could pray toward Mecca. The warden refused—until Malcolm threatened to bring all kinds of political officials into the matter. He said he would contact the Egyptian consul, since Egypt was a country that practiced Islam. He also pointed out that his religious freedom was being denied. Quickly the warden changed his mind and Malcolm got the cells he wanted.

Slowly but surely—perhaps without even knowing it—Malcolm was preparing himself for the life he would eventually lead outside prison.

By preaching Islam to the convicts, he was preparing for his life as a minister and teacher. He was learning how to spread a message of black pride that would win the faith and loyalty of those who came into the Nation of Islam.

By debating in prison, he was preparing for his life as a public speaker. He was learning how to sway a crowd of thousands with the power of his personality, the force of his rich intellect—and his carefully chosen words.

By working to win his rights from the prison officials, he was preparing for his life as a political leader who knew just how far he could go—within the limits of the law.

Years later Malcolm said that his time in prison was a gift from Allah. He said that he was never truly free until he was locked up. Only in prison did he find the freedom to become his own true self.

But by the time Malcolm had been in prison for six years, he was ready to leave. And now he was eligible for parole. He had to ask several times before parole was finally granted in August 1952. Then Malcolm was given a cheap suit and a small amount of money and released. He had been in prison almost six and a half years.

Malcolm the Minister

As soon as twenty-seven-year-old Malcolm was released from prison, he went to live with his brother Wilfred in Detroit, Michigan. Malcolm had no choice. As a paroled prisoner, he was required to have a job, and Wilfred had lined one up for him. It was a job working in the same furniture store that Wilfred worked in. Wilfred was also willing to give Malcolm a place to live.

But more important—as far as Malcolm's brothers and sisters were concerned—Wilfred was a practicing Muslim. He was a member of the Nation of Islam's Temple Number One in Detroit. And Malcolm's family thought it would do him good to spend time with other Muslims. They wanted him to learn more about their religion.

Malcolm was happy to go along with their plan. In fact, everything about the life of a Muslim appealed to him. He liked the orderliness of the ritual prayers. He liked the fact that Muslim men were given so much respect by their families—and that Muslim women were respected by their men. He was thrilled by the warmth and friendship that were openly expressed when Muslims gathered together. He even liked the strict rules that Muslims had to follow.

Being part of the Muslim community was like being part of a strong, supportive, disciplined family—the kind of family Malcolm never had as a child.

The only thing Malcolm didn't like was the size of the temple's membership. Only about forty or fifty people attended the meetings each week. Malcolm wanted to go out into the streets and try to convert more black people to Islam. But Wilfred told him to be patient.

Of course, Malcolm had a hard time being patient. He didn't like to wait for anything. But he decided to keep quiet and wait—for a little while, at least. Soon he was going to have an experience that made everything else seem unimportant. He and the other members of Temple Number One were going to Chicago to see Elijah Muhammad in person!

When the day finally came for the trip, Malcolm eagerly piled into the car with Wilfred and his family. All the other Muslims were lined up to join the caravan, too. It was a hot summer Sunday. Together they drove the 280 miles from Detroit to Chicago and arrived at Temple Number Two. (Each temple was numbered as it was formed. By this time, in 1952, there were ten temples in cities around the country.)

When they got to the Chicago temple, the members greeted them warmly, calling them Brother and Sister. Everyone crowded into the temple and waited for Elijah Muhammad to appear.

Finally the Messenger walked out onto the platform to speak. He was wearing a dark suit, a white shirt, and a bow tie. Malcolm was spellbound from the first moment he saw him. It was, Malcolm said later, the most exciting moment of his life. There he was! Elijah Muhammad himself! He was much smaller and frailer looking than Malcolm had imagined, but that didn't matter. He held Malcolm riveted with his presence and with his words.

For more than an hour Elijah Muhammad spoke about many things. He talked about the "blue-eyed white devils" and about how black people had become "mentally, morally, and spiritually dead" because of the things white people had done. He also talked about his own time in prison. He said he was imprisoned for "teaching the truth" about black people. (In truth, Elijah had actually spent three years in the penitentiary for refusing to register for the draft. The Nation of Islam opposed war, and Elijah was a pacifist, a person who didn't believe in war or violence.)

At the end of his speech Elijah called out Malcolm's name. Malcolm was stunned. The Messenger asked Malcolm to stand up as he told everyone about Malcolm's conversion to Islam in prison. He concluded by challenging Malcolm to remain faithful—now that he was free.

That night all of Wilfred's family were invited to have dinner with Elijah Muhammad at his home. Elijah had just moved into a new eighteen-room mansion in Chicago—a house he said his followers had urged him to buy. The Nation had enough money to support Elijah and his top ministers, using the funds collected at rallies each week.

At dinner that night Elijah tried to draw out Malcolm and the others. He wanted to hear what his guests felt and thought. He treated them in a fatherly way and made them feel at ease. When Malcolm's turn finally came, he was happy to speak up.

"How many members are there supposed to be in our Temple Number One in Detroit?" Malcolm asked.

"There are supposed to be thousands," Elijah replied.

Pleased with the answer, Malcolm then asked the Messenger how to recruit more Muslims. Elijah's answer was simple. He told Malcolm to go after the young people. He said the older people would follow out of shame.

That was all Malcolm needed to hear. As soon as he was back home in Detroit, he began recruiting new members from the streets. It was hard work, but within a few months he had tripled the membership of the Detroit temple.

Meanwhile, Malcolm was waiting to become an official member of the Nation of Islam. He had applied for his new last name—his X. The X stood for the true African family name that each black American had lost during slavery. Since it was nearly impossible for African-Americans to trace their roots and find out their ancestors' names, each new member of the Nation of Islam was given an X instead. The X's were issued from Chicago, from Elijah Muhammad. That way, if there were fourteen Muslims named John, each one would be registered separately. The first one would be John X, then John 2X, and so forth.

Soon Malcolm Little became Malcolm X.

Over the next months and years Malcolm visited Chicago as often as he could to hear Elijah speak. As Elijah got to know Malcolm better, he saw that Malcolm was special. He recognized that Malcolm had the potential to be a good minister. And perhaps he would be a great leader someday. Perhaps he would even take over as leader of the Nation of Islam when Elijah died.

So Elijah gradually gave Malcolm more and more responsibility.

Within a year, by 1953, twenty-eight-year-old Malcolm had become the assistant minister at Temple Number One. A few months later the Messenger sent Malcolm to Boston to start another temple there. Malcolm quit his regular job and from then on devoted himself full-time to the Nation. The Nation paid for all of Malcolm's travel and living expenses. But Malcolm didn't care about the money. All he wanted was to serve the man who had deeply changed his life.

In Boston and elsewhere, Malcolm usually went about recruiting new members in the same way. He would go out into the streets and talk "street talk" with black "brothers," trying to get them interested in the Nation. Then he would hold a meeting in someone's apartment or house. There he would speak about how the white man had robbed the black man of everything—his name, his country, his culture, and most importantly his pride. Finally Malcolm would say:

"Will all stand who *believe* what you have heard."

Usually everyone in the room stood.

Then Malcolm would ask everyone who wanted to *follow* the Honorable Elijah Muhammad to stand.

At this point usually only two or three people stood up.

But little by little Malcolm recruited enough people to form a temple in Boston. It was called Temple Number Eleven. Then Malcolm moved on to Philadelphia and did the same thing all over again. He succeeded in forming a new temple there in just two months.

In many ways Malcolm was following in his father's footsteps. He was doing exactly what Earl Little had done when he preached the ideas of Marcus Garvey so many years before. Constantly on the go, Malcolm traveled from city to city, preaching about black pride. He gathered people together in small groups, sometimes holding meetings at night in living rooms. He talked about the lost African heritage and the need for a separate black nation or state. He encouraged people to leave the white man's world behind and join the Nation of Islam to seek black independence.

And like his father, he would one day be the target of much white hatred. Right now, Malcolm was not so well known to the white community. But soon all that would change.

In April 1954 Malcolm was given a big promotion. He was sent to New York City to become the minister of Temple Number Seven. New York City had a population of nearly one million black Americans. But Temple Number Seven had fewer than fifty members. Malcolm knew that Temple Number Seven had the potential to grow. If he could bring enough new converts into the New York temple, it would certainly get the attention of the media—and the world.

When Malcolm arrived in Harlem, he found that it hadn't changed much since he had been a street hustler there more than ten years before. But Malcolm himself had changed. Now, instead of a zoot suit, he wore a conservative business suit. Instead of conked hair, he let his red hair grow naturally but kept it cut short. In prison his eyesight had weakened—Malcolm thought it was from reading fourteen hours a day. So now he wore glasses, which made him look more serious. He also had grown a small, thin beard.

As a result, during his first weeks back in the old neighborhood, few people recognized Malcolm right away. And Malcolm had a hard time recognizing some of his old buddies. Some of the biggest hustlers had become old, weak, and sick. Others, he heard, were dead.

Still, it was good to see some of the old faces. Malcolm felt good to be returning to Harlem the way he was—so much healthier in body and spirit than when he had left.

But soon Malcolm realized his job in Harlem was going to be tough. The drug addicts, numbers runners, and other hustlers he met on the street were hard to recruit. And there was more competition in Harlem, too. There were many churches and black organizations competing to bring in members.

So Malcolm had to change his tactics. He had to be smart and sly—like the fox in all his favorite fables.

He hung around on the edges of the other group meetings and outside the storefront churches. Then when people were leaving those meetings, he would say, "Come to hear us, too!"

When Malcolm was trying to recruit younger women, he used a different tactic. He talked about how beautiful Muslim women were—because they were loved for their inner beauty and shown true respect by Muslim men.

Over time, his tactics worked. Temple Number Seven grew—not as fast as Malcolm would have liked—but it grew. Not only did the membership increase, but the wealth of the temple grew as well. Eventually the temple collected enough money to start a few small businesses. By 1957 it was a large and important presence in Harlem, although few white people in the rest of New York knew much about it.

Then one day in April something happened that brought Malcolm X—and the Nation of Islam—to the attention of the world.

A Muslim man named Johnson Hinton stopped to watch two police officers who were dealing with a black man—a disruptive drunk—on the streets of Harlem. Hinton and several other people watched in horror as the police beat the drunken man with their clubs.

Soon the police tried to get the onlookers to move away. When Hinton didn't move, the police began beating him, too. Hinton struggled to stop an officer from wielding his nightstick. Then other police officers arrived and joined in. Using their clubs, they beat him to the ground. They handcuffed the bleeding Muslim and took him to the police station. Johnson Hinton had never been arrested before.

Another Muslim man, a friend of Hinton's, ran to a telephone and called a restaurant owned by Temple Seven. From there the word spread. Within thirty minutes many of Malcolm's followers were standing outside the police precinct. They stood peacefully, but in military formation as they had been taught. Many of them were part of a special group of Muslim men called the Fruit of Islam. These men were large and physically fit. They were trained in self-defense to protect the Nation's members and to keep order within the Nation of Islam. They made sure that no one broke the Nation's rules.

As soon as the Muslims appeared on the streets, other residents of Harlem joined them. Almost immediately there were hundreds. Later there were thousands. A terrible angry mood spread throughout the non-Muslim part of the crowd. The police knew a riot could erupt at any moment.

Malcolm went into the police station and asked to see Hinton. At first the police said that Hinton wasn't there. Then they admitted Hinton was there but said Malcolm couldn't see him. The police didn't want to deal with Malcolm—but they didn't know what power he had.

Eventually the officers realized that Malcolm was the only man who could control the crowd. They finally agreed to let him see the beaten man. It was a sight Malcolm never forgot—a picture of pure police brutality. Hinton was covered with blood, and he was only semiconscious. His skull was broken open. Later a steel plate would have to be put in his head.

Sickened by what he saw, Malcolm demanded that Hinton be taken to the hospital and given proper medical care. He also demanded that the police officers involved be punished. The police agreed. In return, they asked Malcolm to help disperse the crowd.

When Malcolm was certain that Hinton would get the medical care he needed, he kept his promise. He stepped out of the station house and without a word simply motioned to the crowd. Immediately the Muslims moved away—and the rest of the crowd followed.

The white police were awestruck.

"No one should have that much power," one white official said.

But Malcolm did have that much power. And now all of New York knew about it. Soon every newspaper and magazine, every radio program and television show, wanted to find out more about the man called Malcolm X.

Three of Malcolm's brothers and sisters outside the Littles' home in Lansing, Michigan. From left to right: Wesley, Yvonne, and Reginald.

Pleasant Grove Elementary School in Lansing, Michigan, where Malcolm attended school.

Malcolm X at age fourteen.

Malcolm's brothers in 1949. From left to right: Philbert, Wesley, Wilfred, and Reginald.

©Eve Arnold/Magnum Photos

Malcolm X, right, with Elijah Muhammad at a rally for the Nation of Islam in 1961.

©1969 John Launois/Black Star

Malcolm and Betty X had six children. Here, Betty holds their third child, Ilyasah.

Malcolm X speaks during a Black Muslim rally in New York City, 1963.

Malcolm visits the Great Pyramids in Egypt during his 1964 trip to the Middle East.

Reporters greet Malcolm at the airport as he returns from his pilgrimage to Mecca. Here he holds his daughter Ilyasah.

Martin Luther King, Jr. and Malcolm X meet at the Capitol in Washington, D.C., 1964.

Malcolm X outside his home after it was hit by two fire bombs in 1965.

Huge crowds such as this one in Harlem, New York City, came to hear Malcolm's powerful speeches.

Two policemen carry Malcolm X from the Audubon Ballroom after he was shot during a rally on February 21, 1965. He was taken to the hospital and pronounced dead on arrival.

Betty X, Malcolm's widow, stands at Malcolm's grave while an Islamic prayer is chanted.

Private Life, Public Life

Malcolm lived almost his entire life in the public eye.

He was always speaking in public or giving public interviews. He was completely comfortable when he was in the public spotlight.

Nearly everything Malcolm did, he did in public. Nearly everything he felt or said was in public.

But he had a few private thoughts. In 1957, for instance, when Temple Number Seven had grown strong, Malcolm privately began to think about marriage.

It wasn't that he was in love with anyone. Not at all. Malcolm was too wrapped up in his work for that. But there was a young Muslim woman named Betty Sanders—called Sister Betty X—whom Malcolm had noticed. She seemed like the kind of woman he would want to marry, if he ever did get married. She was educated, intelligent, and reserved.

Malcolm hadn't spoken to her much when he picked her out of the crowd. He had only seen her at various Muslim meetings. She was a nurse and taught a personal-health class for Muslim women. Sometimes Minister Malcolm would drop in to watch.

Finally one day he asked Betty if she would like to go with him to the Museum of Natural History. It wasn't a date—at least Malcolm didn't think so. He just wanted to show her some educational exhibits. Betty agreed to go.

But at the last minute Malcolm tried to back out. He called to say he was too busy. Betty was clearly annoyed, and she let her feelings show.

"Well, you sure waited long enough to tell me, Brother Minister," she said. "I was just ready to walk out the door."

Feeling bad about changing his mind, Malcolm decided to keep the date after all. Together they explored the museum. The whole time Malcolm quizzed Betty to find out what she was like.

Soon Malcolm found himself thinking about marriage—but the thoughts scared him completely. So he stayed far away from Betty for a long time. Meanwhile, though, he arranged for Betty to go to Chicago to meet Elijah Muhammad. And he was glad to hear that the Messenger thought she was a good Muslim sister.

Then one day in January 1958 Malcolm got in his car and drove from New York to Detroit to visit his brother Wilfred. By now Wilfred was the minister of Detroit's Temple Number One.

But as soon as Malcolm got to Detroit, he stopped at a pay phone and called Betty, who was back in New York. When she came to the phone, Malcolm just blurted out his message.

"Look, do you want to get married?" he asked.

Betty was surprised, but she said yes. So Malcolm told her to fly out to Detroit right away. After meeting Betty's parents, Malcolm drove her to Lansing and they were married on January 14 by a justice of the peace.

It hadn't been a very romantic courtship. Malcolm didn't believe in all that "mushy" stuff. And it wasn't a very romantic marriage. With Malcolm gone much of the time, traveling all over the United States, Betty hardly ever saw her famous husband. But there was a deep respect between them, which later grew into something that Malcolm would call love. She was one of the few women he ever felt he could really trust.

Over the years they had six children. The first girl was born in November 1958 and was named Attallah, after Attila the Hun. His second daughter, born in December of 1960, was named Qubilah, after Kublai Khan, a fierce ruler of China. (Malcolm used the Chinese spelling of Kublai Khan's name.) Then came Ilyasah, his third child, in 1962. She was given the Arabic name for Elijah. His fourth daughter, Gamilah Lamumbah, was born in 1964. She was named for the murdered African Patrice Lumumba. In 1965, Betty gave birth to their fifth and sixth children, twin daughters named Malaak and Malikah.

Meanwhile, Malcolm's life was growing more and more public every day. First of all, he was now known and recognized by nearly everyone in Harlem. People who had previously paid little attention to the Nation of Islam were now willing to join—because of Malcolm. He was a hero for having stood up to the police on behalf of Johnson Hinton. And he was a leader who could stand up to the white press as well.

Most important, Malcolm electrified his audiences when he spoke. His steady, strong voice and powerful words made it clear that he had no question in his heart about what was right and what was wrong for black Americans. Malcolm said later in his autobiography that his goal was to tell white people about their crimes—and to tell black people the truth. Black Americans were thrilled to hear the words that Malcolm spoke. It made them proud to know that a black person could stand up to white America and say such bold and angry things. No one had ever dared to do that before.

Reporters swarmed around Malcolm. Some wanted to hear him talk about the "white, blue-eyed devils." They were obviously looking for angry, attention-getting words to put in print—words that would help sell magazines by alarming the white population. Other reporters were truly trying to understand the Nation's message.

But in 1959 a television documentary established how the world would think of the Nation. The program was a television documentary called *The Hate That Hate Produced.* It had been filmed with Elijah Muhammad's cooperation, but the final program was not one that the Nation of Islam liked. It was edited to produce a shocking effect, and it succeeded. White Americans were horrified to hear Malcolm explain that Elijah believed all white people were devils. The program focused on the fact that the Nation—or "Black Muslims," as the press began calling the members—seemed to be teaching *hate*.

After that, Malcolm X was at the center of a lot of media attention. Debates and panel discussions were held on television so that Malcolm could explain—and defend—his views. Of course, Malcolm had a lot of experience debating. Years ago in prison he had learned to win arguments through the power of clear reasoning and the sheer force of his will. He was also very smart and clever in conversations. He could turn a conversation or a debate whichever way he wanted.

And he was a supreme master of the art of answering a question with a question.

For instance, when he was asked why the Fruit of Islam were being trained in judo and karate, Malcolm didn't answer the question directly. Instead he asked his own question:

"Why does judo or karate seem so threatening just because black men are studying it?"

He often silenced his opponents in this way. His answers were good, and the points he made were often reasonable.

But the more Malcolm appeared in public, the more strongly people felt about him—both for and against.

At one point Malcolm said, "I rejoice when a white man dies!" Another time he said that Allah had brought him "good news" when 120 white people died in a plane crash.

Malcolm also talked about the day when black people would rise up in violence against their white enemies. He said that hostility was good—and that he wanted people to get out of control.

He also said that all thoughtful white people "know they are inferior to black people."

These quotes were often reported in the press as single statements. The rest of what Malcolm said was often left out.

Whenever Malcolm talked of violence, he was very careful. He didn't actually *tell* his followers to go out and commit acts of violence against whites. But he said that black people were very likely to "lose control" if they didn't get what they deserved.

He made it sound as if he approved of violence. At one point a white minister was killed during a protest in Cleveland, Ohio, in support of black schoolchildren. Instead of showing sympathy for the minister, Malcolm said, "It's time that some white people started dying in this thing!"

And in some of his most famous speeches, Malcolm said that black Americans should have the right to regain their rights as human beings by any means necessary. That phrase—*by any means necessary*—became a symbol of Malcolm's anger at white Americans.

When reporters tried to pin Malcolm down about his attitudes toward violence, Malcolm wouldn't answer directly. He wouldn't say yes, he favored violence. And he wouldn't say no either.

The private Malcolm was very unlikely to commit an act of violence. How could he? He was a gentle man who, unlike his father, had never lifted a hand against his children or his wife. He was also surprisingly friendly and well mannered to the white reporters who interviewed him—considering that he said they were devils.

But the public Malcolm sounded so angry that he inflamed the emotions of thousands of people. Many of his followers believed that he was encouraging them to take out their anger on the whites of the world.

Very few people, either black or white, understood that there was a difference between what Malcolm said and what he personally would actually do.

In public Malcolm called himself "the angriest Negro in America." And just about everyone agreed. Even many black leaders of the civil-rights movement were shocked by the things Malcolm said.

The Reverend Dr. Martin Luther King, Jr., for instance, felt that Malcolm's angry language was dividing the black community and hurting their cause.

But Malcolm made it clear that he did not approve of the nonviolent ways of Martin Luther King. He saw what happened when King's followers marched or staged sit-ins at rallies in the South, trying to achieve their civil rights. Sometimes the police came out and beat the marchers with sticks. Other times the National Guard came and used tear gas. Malcolm thought it was ridiculous for black people to sit passively and take that kind of abuse. To him it was just more of the same abuse that white slave owners and their descendants had dished out for more than three hundred years.

As the years went by, however, some of Malcolm's

friends thought he may have secretly admired Martin Luther King. Perhaps he even envied him. King was loved and admired by many more people than Malcolm was. People criticized Malcolm, but they praised King. There may have been a part of Malcolm that wanted to be accepted the way King was—and understood as well.

Most of all, Malcolm might have envied the fact that King was actively involved in politics. King had led many of the civil-rights marches in the South in the 1950s and 1960s. He had been there when black Americans staged a boycott of the buses in Montgomery, Alabama. He led civil-rights protests in Birmingham, Alabama, and helped bring 200,000 people to a march on Washington, D.C.

Malcolm deeply wanted to join the political movement, too. He longed to use the Nation's power and voice to help the civil-rights movement go forward. But Elijah Muhammad forbade Malcolm and all his followers to take political action. Malcolm was allowed to *talk* about his political views—but he wasn't allowed to organize his followers. He couldn't join protest marches, or register people to vote, or get involved in any other kind of public political stand.

Publicly, Malcolm obeyed. But privately, he felt uneasy.

How could he just stand by and do nothing when the world was on the verge of a dramatic and important change?

Several years later, in 1964, Malcolm and Martin Luther King met. They were both visiting the U.S. Senate in Washington, D.C. Dr. King was giving a news conference, and photographers were there. As King moved into a hallway, Malcolm quickly stepped into his path.

"Well, Malcolm, good to see you," Dr. King said.

"Good to see *you*," Malcolm said with a grin.

Photographers took pictures as the two men shook hands. It was the only time Malcolm and Martin came face to face.

Leaving Elijah

By 1963, Malcolm had risen to be the most well-known member of the Muslim community. His Temple Number Seven was now really three New York temples—one in Harlem, one in Queens, and one in Brooklyn. Malcolm was also Elijah Muhammad's right-hand man. Whenever Elijah spoke at rallies, it was Malcolm who was chosen to introduce him. But the introductions were more like speeches of their own. Malcolm was the man who could excite the audiences and fire up their emotions. When Elijah could not speak, Malcolm always spoke in his place.

There were other signs of Malcolm's power, too. For instance, he was named as the Nation of Islam's first National Minister. And he had almost unlimited access to the Nation's funds. The Nation even bought Malcolm a car and paid for his house.

Malcolm didn't think much of these privileges. He saw himself as nothing more than a servant to the Messenger. He knew he would never take advantage of the money or power—because the only things that mattered to him were his faith in Elijah and his faith in Islam.

In fact, Malcolm often said that he was willing to die for Elijah.

So it surprised Malcolm when things began to happen that would rip the two men apart.

First of all, there was no way to keep people from being jealous of Malcolm. Malcolm *was* the brightest star in the organization. He *did* get all the media attention. And more important, he *was* Elijah's favorite for years. Even though Elijah had children of his own, Malcolm was treated like a favorite son. Elijah's own sons and daughters had less important roles.

Sometimes it even seemed to Malcolm that Elijah was jealous of him.

But jealousy wasn't the only problem.

Malcolm himself was feeling restless. He wanted to be more politically active, to get involved with civil rights. But Elijah wouldn't allow it. Elijah did not want the Nation of Islam to seem like a radical group.

The final problem, however, was Elijah himself—because slowly Malcolm began to realize that Elijah Muhammad had sinned.

The rumors had been around for years. People close to Elijah said that he had had romances with his secretaries, and children had been born out of wedlock.

But for quite some time Malcolm refused to believe these rumors. He did not want to admit to himself that the man he worshipped was merely human—that the Messenger of Allah could make human mistakes. It was especially shocking to Malcolm because the Nation's rules about moral behavior were so strict.

And Malcolm had another reason for not wanting to believe that Elijah was flawed. Malcolm's entire life was wrapped up in the Nation of Islam. His entire identity depended on being a Muslim. If Malcolm abandoned the Nation of Islam, what would he do? Who would he be?

On the other hand, how could he go on preaching the "truths" about Elijah if Elijah had broken this rule?

As Malcolm later said in his autobiography, it took him many months to face the truth. When he finally did, he felt deeply betrayed.

He sent a letter to Elijah, confronting him with the rumors. Elijah didn't answer in writing. Instead he called Malcolm and told him that they could talk about it the next time they were together.

The meeting came soon enough—in April 1963. Malcolm flew to Phoenix, Arizona, to see Elijah, who had moved there for his health.

In the meeting, Elijah and Malcolm talked outside near his swimming pool. Perhaps Elijah did not want anyone else to hear. With only Malcolm listening, he practically confessed that he was guilty.

Malcolm was horrified. He felt shaken to the bottom of his soul by this revelation. And worse, he felt like a fool. Was this the man Malcolm had said he would die for?

Now Malcolm had a problem that was almost too big for him to solve.

Basically, Malcolm had become a very honest man. He could not go on living a lie—pretending that he did not know about Elijah's wrongdoings.

But at the same time, he was not ready to leave the Nation of Islam. Not yet. He was too attached to his work in the Nation, and to his identity as its leader. It was too hard to give that up.

Over the next few months Malcolm did a number of things to anger Elijah—things that finally forced Elijah to throw Malcolm out.

First Malcolm told a number of other ministers about Elijah's sins, and soon the news was reported in the press. It was rumored that Malcolm himself had leaked the news.

Then Malcolm found many little ways to disobey his spiritual leader. Although Elijah had always told Malcolm to stay out of politics, Malcolm disobeyed. He worked to register voters in Harlem. He supported a multiracial labor union. And he urged his followers to support an all-black political party called Freedom Now.

The final straw, though, came in November 1963, when President John F. Kennedy was shot. Elijah quickly told all his ministers to say nothing about the assassination. Malcolm was under strict orders to say only "No comment."

But Malcolm could not keep quiet. He gave a speech just a few days after the assassination. When someone in the audience asked what he thought of Kennedy's death, Malcolm said that it seemed like a case of "the chickens coming home to roost." What he meant was that all the violent acts white people had committed against blacks over the years were now coming back—or "coming home"—to the race of people who had committed them. Instead of expressing grief that the president was dead, Malcolm seemed to feel that the assassination was okay—that it was a kind of justice for the crimes white people had committed in the past.

Elijah was furious. He knew that the country had loved Kennedy. He knew, too, that Malcolm's statement would make the Nation of Islam look bad.

So Elijah decided to "silence" Malcolm for ninety days.

That meant no talking to the press. No preaching in his own temples. Nothing.

As if to embarrass him further, Elijah told the press that Malcolm had been silenced. Big headlines in the newspapers proclaimed that Malcolm X was no longer in favor.

For a while Malcolm hoped that he would eventually be reinstated to the Nation. But in his heart he knew his time in the Nation was over. He had angered and betrayed Elijah—and he felt betrayed in return. There was no way they could go on together, like father and son, as they had before.

On His Own

Soon Malcolm began to hear talk about death threats. There were rumors that the Nation of Islam wanted him dead. And the death threats weren't just talk.

One of Malcolm's close assistants in Temple Number Seven gave the order to have him killed. A man named Langston X was supposed to wire Malcolm's car with explosives so that it would explode when Malcolm turned the key to start the car. But instead Langston came to Malcolm and told him about the plot.

"I thanked him for my life," Malcolm wrote in his autobiography.

From that moment on, Malcolm knew that he was marked for death. He could never return to the Nation of Islam now. There was too much bad blood between him and Elijah Muhammad.

There was only one thing to do. He would start his own organization to help change the destiny of black Americans.

Why not? Malcolm thought. There had always been thousands of people in Harlem who wanted to follow him—ever since he had fearlessly faced the police when Johnson Hinton was beaten. But many people had been turned off by the strict rules of the Nation of Islam. Maybe Malcolm could recruit them now. Maybe he could bring them into a *new* temple, or mosque, as they were now called. The new mosque would be open to black people of all faiths. It wouldn't be quite so strict.

Malcolm called a press conference to announce that he was leaving the Nation of Islam. He said he was starting his own mosque called Muslim Mosque, Inc. He knew that he would have some loyal followers who would leave the Nation to join him. Langston X and others from Temple Number Seven had already pledged their loyalty to Malcolm.

Still, going off on his own was a big step. It would take all his strength and courage to go on leading people without the moral and emotional support of the man who had been like a father to him.

Maybe that's why Malcolm felt there was something else he needed to do first. First he wanted to make a pilgrimage to Mecca.

Mecca is the holy city of Islam, located in Saudi Arabia. For centuries it has been an obligation of all Muslims to make a pilgrimage to Mecca at least once in their lifetime, if they are able. The pilgrimage is called a *hajj*. It involves performing a number of rituals, or religious acts. These are performed in the city and at the ancient temple called the Ka'ba.

Malcolm wanted to make his pilgrimage now—now that he had been separated from the Nation of Islam. After all, the Nation had given him spiritual guidance ever since he had been in prison. But now Malcolm wanted to learn about the *true* Islam, so that he would have a spiritual base for the work he planned to do in years to come.

There were two problems, though. Malcolm had very little money of his own since leaving the Nation— not enough to pay for a trip. And it was very hard for an American to get permission to visit Mecca. Only true Muslims were permitted inside the holy city.

Malcolm went to the Saudi Arabian ambassador in New York to ask for a visa. But he was told there was only one way to get a visa to visit Mecca. He would need to get a letter of approval from a man named Dr. Mahmoud Shawarbi.

Dr. Shawarbi was a professor from the University of Cairo in Egypt who now lived in New York. He was also a well-known authority on Islamic matters in the United States.

Malcolm called Dr. Shawarbi, hoping that he could somehow persuade him to help.

To Malcolm's surprise Dr. Shawarbi said, "I was just going to get in touch with you! Come right over!"

When Malcolm got there, Dr. Shawarbi handed him a book. It was a gift from an Egyptian named Abd ar-Rahman Azzam, who lived in Saudi Arabia. Mr. Azzam was an author who knew of Malcolm's reputation in America. Azzam was interested in this unusual American Muslim and wanted Shawarbi to give Malcolm a copy of his book.

Shawarbi also gave Malcolm the letter he needed so Malcolm could visit Mecca. Then he gave him something else: two telephone numbers. One was the number of Shawarbi's son, who lived in Cairo. The other was the number of Azzam's son, who lived in Jidda. Jidda was the Saudi Arabian city Malcolm would have to pass through on his way to Mecca.

The only problem remaining was the question of money. How could Malcolm afford to pay for this expensive trip? He turned to the one person who had always wanted him to succeed—his half-sister Ella. Ella was now a Muslim herself, and she had broken away from the Nation, too. She had been saving money to make her own pilgrimage to Mecca. But instead she gave the money to Malcolm. She felt that it was more important for him to go.

To make the *hajj*, Malcolm flew from New York to Frankfurt, in Germany. Then he boarded a second plane headed for Cairo.

From the moment he stepped onto the second plane, he began to feel he was in a different world. Nearly everyone on the plane was a Muslim! They were all making the same pilgrimage he was. At once, Malcolm later said, he felt surrounded by a kind of warmth and acceptance and understanding. Every person, no matter what color skin, seemed to share a kind of brotherhood with the other Muslims. It didn't matter that some of them were blue-eyed and blond-haired . . . or that others had brown skin . . . or that others were black. All treated one another with a sense of friendship and respect that Malcolm had never experienced before.

It was hard for Malcolm to believe, but every person seemed concerned for his welfare. Malcolm felt that Allah was watching over him on this important trip.

After sightseeing in Cairo for two days, it was time to fly to Jidda. Malcolm had met a group of Muslims who spoke English, so he drove to the Cairo airport with them. They showed him how to prepare for the pilgrimage. First, he had to take off his clothes and put on just two white towels. One towel was wrapped around his waist. The other was worn on his shoulders. On his feet Malcolm wore very thin sandals. All the pilgrims leaving Cairo were dressed this way. The airport was filled with thousands and thousands of people, all dressed for the *hajj*.

On the plane to Jidda, Malcolm was again thrilled by the sense of brotherhood he saw among people of every color. And everyone treated him as if he were special because he was an *American* Muslim. An American Muslim, after all, was a very unusual thing.

But when he arrived in Jidda, Malcolm's good fortune began to run out. In the Jidda airport each pilgrim had to pass through customs. When Malcolm showed his American passport to the customs official, the man would not let him go through.

Frantically Malcolm's new Muslim friends tried to persuade the customs officials to allow him into the country. They argued in Arabic. They showed the letter from Dr. Shawarbi.

But it was no use. The officials said that Malcolm would have to go before a Muslim high court to prove that he was a sincere Muslim. It was the government's way of making sure that no non-Muslim would ever enter the holy city.

So Malcolm was separated from his friends and led to a huge building at the airport. The building was like a dormitory. It was packed with people from all over the world. Everywhere Malcolm turned, he saw Muslims from all nations. But none of them were American, and none spoke English.

A young Arab who spoke no English showed Malcolm to a small room. With gestures the Arab told Malcolm that this was where he would have to stay. The room was filled with about fifteen other people, all sitting or sleeping on their prayer rugs. Malcolm tried to pray but found that he did not know the correct prayer positions that true Muslims used. He also did not know how to say the prayers in Arabic. It was a humbling experience—and Malcolm began to feel like a true pilgrim after all.

Would he ever see Mecca?

Suddenly Malcolm remembered something. The telephone numbers! Dr. Shawarbi had given him the number of Mr. Azzam's son. And Omar Azzam lived right there in Jidda!

Quickly he phoned Omar, who came straight to the airport. Within half an hour Malcolm was on his way to the Azzams' house.

The next few days were a whirlwind of exciting events. First Malcolm was invited to stay in Omar Azzam's father's luxurious suite at the Jidda Palace Hotel. Malcolm couldn't believe the generosity. Then a wonderful dinner was given in his honor by the Azzams, who treated him like a brother and a son. Malcolm felt overwhelmed by the honor.

In fact, as he later said in his autobiography, that day was the start of a "radical alteration" in his whole outlook toward white people. He *had* to change his mind—because from Malcolm's point of view the Azzams were white! Their complexions were so light that in America he felt they would have been called white.

But they were not behaving the way he expected white people to behave. They were warm and generous to him. They gave him every honor, and every courtesy, and expected nothing in return.

From that moment on Malcolm changed his way of thinking. He no longer believed that all white people were the enemy. In fact, he began to feel that it was possible to have a true sense of brotherhood with white people in America—if white Americans would change their attitudes and behavior toward blacks.

The next morning the Azzams arranged for Malcolm to go before the high court. After answering a few questions about his faith, Malcolm was accepted as a true Muslim. Finally he could go on to Mecca!

Then came one of the most exciting moments of all. Malcolm was told that a private chauffeured car would be sent to take him on the *hajj*. The car was being sent by Prince Faisal, the highest leader in the land. Why? Because Omar Azzam's sister was married to the prince's son!

Malcolm X was being treated like royalty—by royalty.

The pilgrimage itself was astonishing to Malcolm. He could not believe how many Muslims there were in Mecca. Thousands of pilgrims were performing the ritual of walking around the Ka'ba. Thousands more were sitting, sleeping, or praying. Because of the crowds, Malcolm could not get near the ancient black stone of the Ka'ba to kiss it—a traditional part of the *hajj*. But he did cry out *Takbir!*, which means "God is great!" Then he and thousands of other Muslims walked to Mount Arafat, a hill about fifteen miles from Mecca. Malcolm felt one with the great mass of faithful Muslims who had come together to express their deep faith in Allah.

After the *hajj*, Malcolm was again honored in a way that he would never forget. He was invited to have a private meeting with Prince Faisal himself! The prince was warm and friendly to Malcolm—as nearly everyone else in this part of the world had been. But Prince Faisal did want Malcolm to know one thing— that the teachings of Elijah Muhammad were not the true Islam.

Malcolm heard the same thing from other Muslims during his trip. They all assured him that the teachings of Elijah Muhammad were not the true Muslim religion.

From Saudi Arabia, Malcolm began a tour of other nations in the Middle East and Africa. This part of the trip became one of the most important experiences in his life.

First Malcolm went to Beirut, in Lebanon, and spoke at the university there. After the speech students swarmed around him, asking for autographs. From Beirut he traveled on to Egypt briefly.

Then Malcolm made his way to Nigeria, a country that had recently fought for and won its independence.

In Nigeria, Malcolm was an honored speaker at Ibadan University. There he began to spread his message about the need for unity between black people in America and Africa. Malcolm felt that Africa's newly independent nations were struggling for some of the same rights and freedoms that black people in America were fighting for. He urged the independent African nations to help their brothers and sisters in America by bringing civil-rights issues to the attention of the United Nations.

From Nigeria, Malcolm flew on to Ghana, where he met with about forty well-known black Americans who had chosen to live in Africa for a while. Among them were authors Maya Angelou and Julian Mayfield. Together they talked about the civil-rights struggle and what they could all do to help.

Reporters followed Malcolm everywhere in Ghana. Again, he was received like royalty. He met with ambassadors and other important diplomats and heads of state. Again and again great dinners were given in his honor.

Wherever Malcolm went in Africa, he was treated with enormous respect for his leadership of black people in America. It was quite a change from the way he had been treated back home.

The tour of the African nations had a profound effect on Malcolm. He came away from it with a strong sense of the brotherhood between all people of color in the world. He especially saw a connection between the needs of black people in America and those in Africa. And to Malcolm's delight, the Africans encouraged him to think that way. They told him that the word *Negro*—which was the most accepted word for black people in America at the time—was not favored in Africa. "The word *Afro-American* has greater meaning and dignity," they said.

By this, they meant that they welcomed all black Americans to feel connected to their African heritage.

Malcolm felt as if his eyes had been opened to a whole new way of thinking. A new way of thinking about black Americans . . . about Islam . . . about race and color . . . a new way of thinking about the world.

Now he just had to return to America and find a way to put this new thinking to work. But as it turned out, that was not such a simple thing to do.

Another Fire

When Malcolm returned to New York in May 1964 after six weeks away, everyone was waiting for him.

His wife, Betty, and his children had missed him very much. They were ecstatic to have him back home.

But his followers, it seemed, had missed him even more. The Muslims who had broken away from Elijah to join Malcolm felt utterly lost in his absence. They did not know what to do—or even what to think—without Malcolm around. And his new organization, the Muslim Mosque, Inc., had barely gotten off the ground. It certainly could not grow without Malcolm there.

And then there were the reporters—dozens of them. People from the press and radio and television were all waiting to hear what the "new" Malcolm X would say. They already knew that his views had begun to change because Malcolm had mailed them a letter from Mecca saying so. Now he told the press that he was changing his name, too. He was now calling himself El-Hajj Malik El-Shabazz.

"Malcolm! Are you saying that you no longer think

all white people are evil?" the reporters called out at a press conference.

"True, sir!" Malcolm replied. "I have adjusted my thinking to the point where I believe that whites are human beings!" He stopped—then added, "As long as this is borne out by their humane attitude toward Negroes."

All of a sudden there was a new Malcolm X to deal with. But the problem was that no one seemed to want a "new" Malcolm X. His old followers began to wonder whether he was still as tough and strong as he used to be. After all, he wasn't talking as tough as he had in the old days.

The press, on the other hand, did not seem to believe that Malcolm had really changed. They still wrote stories about his anger and his support of violence. They still blamed him when violence erupted in the city streets.

And Malcolm himself did not seem to know quite what he believed. It was hard for him to express his new feelings without losing his old followers. So he tried to do both. He tried to tell his followers from the ghetto that he still believed in strong actions against white racism. And then he tried to tell the moderate black leaders—people such as Martin Luther King—that he was changing, that he was trying to help. In the long run he found he was stuck with his old image, and neither side believed him.

For the next few months Malcolm floundered. He tried to start yet another organization. This one was called the Organization of Afro-American Unity. It was patterned after a similar organization in Africa, the Organization of African Unity. But as soon as he had announced its formation, he left the country again—maybe because he didn't know what to do next. This time he spent eighteen weeks away, and when he came back, his new organization was on the verge of falling apart.

In the meantime, the death threats against Malcolm continued. Wherever Malcolm went, Black Muslims were there. They seemed to be watching him, following him, from city to city. Death threats were telephoned to his home, to his offices, and even to the police. When he was out of town, the Black Muslims knew where he was staying and showed up at his hotel.

Malcolm fought back with the best weapon he had—his mouth. He told everyone that the Black Muslims were trying to kill him. He also began attacking Elijah Muhammad in the press.

By now there was almost open warfare between Malcolm and Elijah Muhammad. But Elijah seemed to have all the power. And one of his biggest weapons was the fact that the Nation of Islam still owned Malcolm's house.

Years before, when Malcolm was in favor, Elijah had generously bought the house for Malcolm. He planned to give it to Malcolm outright and encouraged Malcolm to put the house in his own name. But Malcolm had refused. He did not want it to look as if he were profiting from the Nation. He told Betty, "Don't worry. If anything happens to me, I know that the Nation will take care of my family."

Now Elijah was trying to take the house back.

The Nation of Islam got a court order saying that Malcolm and his family had to move. Malcolm appealed the decision, but he lost. Soon the judge would order them to get out—even if they had nowhere else to live.

It was similar to what had happened when Malcolm was a child and his family was ordered to leave their house. Malcolm must have felt it was just as unfair, too.

Then the night before Malcolm was to go to court about it one last time, something happened. There was a commotion in the middle of the night. People were shouting. And once again Malcolm's house was on fire!

Malcolm managed to get Betty and the children out of the house unharmed. But almost all their possessions burned.

Afterward, Malcolm blamed the Black Muslims for the fire. He said they had thrown homemade bombs through the windows from outside.

But the police told another story. They said Malcolm had started the fire—for revenge. The police claimed that Malcolm was trying to destroy the house since he knew he couldn't keep it.

To this day, no one knows for sure what happened. Perhaps Malcolm's enemies started the fire. Some people thought the FBI might have been involved. The FBI had been watching Malcolm and following him. They had even tapped his telephone. In many ways they considered him an enemy.

Or maybe Malcolm set the fire himself. Maybe he

was doing what his own father had been accused of doing years before. Perhaps it was the only way he could think of to grab at some kind of justice.

In any case, the police did not arrest Malcolm. Seven days later he was dead.

Assassination

In the days following the fire Malcolm was hardly himself. For the first time in his life he seemed to have regrets.

He told Betty that he was sorry he had left her alone so much and that he wouldn't do it again.

He told a photographer that he regretted some of the things he had said and done years before. Once, in the early 1960s, a young white college student had come to Malcolm. She had heard him speak at her college, and she desperately wanted to help with his cause. Malcolm had been very harsh with her, telling her there was nothing she could do. Now he was sorry he had treated her that way.

And in several ways Malcolm seemed to regret having spent twelve years of his life devoted to the Nation of Islam.

But the biggest change in Malcolm was that he seemed to know that his own death was coming—and he was resigned to it. He even talked about it with Alex Haley, the journalist who was writing Malcolm's autobiography. Before the fire, Malcolm told Haley that he didn't expect to live long enough to see the book in final form.

Now he told a friend that he had been "marked for death" within the next five days.

On Saturday, February 20, 1965, Malcolm and Betty spent some time together picking out a new house. Then he said good-bye to her and left her and the children with friends on Long Island, New York.

Alone and weary, Malcolm drove into New York City and checked into a hotel. He was tired, and as he had told Alex Haley a few weeks before, his nerves were shot. He needed some rest. He especially needed to build up his energy because the next day he would be speaking at a rally in Harlem. Malcolm had rented the Audubon Ballroom for a fund-raising meeting. Other important black leaders were supposed to be there, too. Malcolm knew that he was running out of time to get his own organization together. Maybe this would be his last chance.

At eight o'clock the next morning the telephone in Malcolm's hotel room rang. Malcolm answered it and a man said, "Wake up, brother." Then the man hung up.

Malcolm knew that the end was near. He called Ella and told her. Then he called Betty and asked her to bring the children and come to the meeting in Harlem. She was surprised but pleased. Malcolm had told her just the day before that she wasn't allowed to come.

When Malcolm arrived at the Audubon Ballroom around one-thirty on Sunday afternoon, some of the crowd was already there. They were sitting in the front rows, waiting for the meeting to start. They had slipped in even before Malcolm's bodyguards had arrived.

In years past, when Malcolm was still with Elijah, no one had ever been allowed to enter a rally without being searched. In those days there were bodyguards everywhere. Security was tight. But not now.

Now Malcolm was waiting for death to come. He had a man in charge of security but told him not to search the crowd. He had been offered extra protection by the police, but according to the police, he told them to keep most of their men outside.

"If I can't be safe among my own kind, where can I be?" he said.

The meeting was supposed to start at two o'clock sharp. But as two o'clock approached, Malcolm realized that none of the other black leaders were coming. They had all called to cancel, except one who didn't even bother to call. Malcolm felt so unhappy that he lost his temper and snapped at a young woman who worked for him.

Finally at two o'clock Malcolm sent one of his aides onstage to begin the meeting. Benjamin X, one of Malcolm's assistants, spoke for about half an hour and then introduced Malcolm, who was waiting backstage.

"The way I feel, I ought not to go out there at all today," Malcolm told the young woman he had snapped at.

But everyone was waiting for him. The crowd was clapping loudly. Malcolm stood up and apologized to the young woman for having spoken harshly to her earlier in the day.

Quickly she reassured him that it was nothing. "I understand," she said.

"I wonder if anybody really understands," he replied, his voice sounding far away.

Then he walked onto the stage and greeted the crowd with the Arabic words that were spoken at the start of every Muslim meeting. But before he could even begin his speech, there was a disturbance in the crowd.

"Take your hand out of my pocket!" a man's angry voice cried.

As nearly every face in the auditorium turned to see what was going on, three men stood up in the front row and began firing at Malcolm X.

The disturbance in the crowd had been a phony distraction. And it worked. Malcolm's bodyguards were drawn away from their leader. Soon there was so much chaos that no one knew what was happening.

No one knew exactly how many gunmen rushed the stage.

But the first bullets to hit Malcolm seemed to come from a sawed-off, double-barreled shotgun. They struck him in the heart. Malcolm reached up to clutch his chest. But the assassins kept firing. As if in slow motion Malcolm fell backward, knocking over some chairs. The gunmen continued to shoot, even after he was down.

When it was over, there were more than a dozen bullet holes in the dead leader, who lay bleeding on the floor.

Several people jumped onto the stage and tried to

revive him. Overwrought, Betty ran forward, too. "My husband!" she cried. "They're killing my husband!"

With people screaming and shouting, the assassins tried to escape. One—or maybe more—did get away. But one man, a Muslim named Talmadge Hayer, was caught. He was grabbed by the crowd, then shot in the leg by one of Malcolm's men. Hayer tried to shoot back, then hurled himself down the stairs leading to the entrance. But the crowd was wild. They were furious. They grabbed at him and kicked him. A moment later two police officers appeared and took Hayer away.

News of Malcolm's death spread rapidly around Harlem and throughout the world. Nearly everyone said the Nation of Islam had killed him. And some people thought that the police knew he was going to be shot—and they just let it happen.

In foreign nations Malcolm was hailed as a martyr and a hero. At home, twenty thousand New Yorkers came to Harlem to see his body and to mourn his death.

During his lifetime Malcolm had accomplished many things. He transformed himself into a deeply moral, spiritual person and lifted himself out of a life of drug addiction, self-hatred, and poverty. He restored a sense of pride in their African heritage to thousands—perhaps millions—of black Americans. He offered America his own view of civil-rights issues—and it was different from the views held by

Martin Luther King and other black leaders who were thought to be more moderate. As Malcolm often said, white Americans probably found it easier to accept Martin Luther King after they had heard Malcolm X speak! And he gave a voice to the powerful and painful anger felt by millions of black people who had been the victims of racism throughout their lives.

At the time of his death, thirty-nine-year-old Malcolm was groping for a better understanding of how black Americans could express their anger—without separating from the whole of American society. He was talking about organizing black Americans to vote in one solid group, and about international cooperation between Africans and black Americans. He was discussing economic power. He spoke of acceptance of peoples of all faiths.

If he had lived, many people think he would have become one of the most powerful political figures this nation has known.

But he did not live, and for a long time white Americans remembered only one thing. They remembered that at the height of his anger Malcolm X said that white people were devils. It was such a powerful, frightening, and negative statement that it prevented the rest of his message from being heard.

At his funeral the actor Ossie Davis, who had known Malcolm well, gave a moving and beautiful speech. In it he explained why Malcolm meant so much to the people he had led. He stated:

"Malcolm was our manhood, our living black manhood! This was his meaning to his people. And in honoring him, we honor the best in ourselves. . . . We will know him then for what he was and is—a Prince— our own shining black Prince!—who didn't hesitate to die, because he loved us so."

Malcolm X

1925 Malcolm Little is born on May 19 in Omaha, Nebraska. His parents, Earl and Louise Little, eventually settle in Michigan.

1929 Malcolm's childhood home in Lansing, Michigan, burns to the ground. His father is accused of having set the fire, but Earl Little claims that white racists did it. Malcolm is only four years old.

1931 When Malcolm is six, his father is run over by a streetcar and dies.

1939 Louise Little is committed to a mental hospital and Malcolm is sent to live in a juvenile-detention home.

1941 At the age of fifteen, Malcolm leaves Michigan and goes to live with his half-sister Ella in Boston. Here he slowly becomes involved with drugs and other illegal activities.

1945– Malcolm and his friends burglarize several pri-
1946 vate homes. Eventually Malcolm is arrested and convicted of burglary. He is sentenced to ten years in prison.

1948– Slowly Malcolm becomes converted to the Na-
1949 tion of Islam while in prison. He writes to the Honorable Elijah Muhammad, leader of the Nation of Islam, asking for guidance with his religious training. He also begins to educate himself by reading hundreds of books from the prison library.

1952 On August 7, Malcolm is paroled after more than six years in prison. He moves in with his brother Wilfred and begins to attend the Nation of Islam's Temple Number One in Detroit. Within a few weeks Malcolm meets Elijah Muhammad in person and is deeply moved by the experience. A few months later he changes his name to Malcolm X.

1954 Malcolm is appointed minister of Temple Number Seven in New York City.

1957 When a Muslim named Johnson Hinton is beaten by police in Harlem, Malcolm leads the black community in protest. The episode demonstrates Malcolm's power as a leader and helps to build his following in Harlem.

1958 On January 14, Malcolm marries Betty Sanders, who is also called Sister Betty X. Over the years they will have six children.

1959 A television program called *The Hate That Hate Produced* is aired in New York City. It brings nationwide media attention to Malcolm X and to the Nation of Islam. The press begins to call the Nation's members "Black Muslims."

1963 In April, Malcolm confronts Elijah Muhammad about rumors that Elijah has committed adultery. According to Malcolm, Elijah admits his sins. In November, President John F. Kennedy is assassinated. Soon after, Malcolm makes a speech in which he says that the president's death is a case of "the chickens coming home to roost." Angry with Malcolm's statement, Elijah silences him for the next ninety days.

1964 Malcolm holds a press conference in March to announce that he has broken away from the Nation of Islam. In April and May he makes a pilgrimage to the holy city of Mecca and then tours several African nations. During the trip he changes his name to El-Hajj Malik El-Shabazz. In June Malcolm forms a group called the Organization of Afro-American Unity. Meanwhile, the Nation of Islam demands that Malcolm and his family move out of their house, which is owned by the Nation. Malcolm stalls, hoping his lawyer can win when he appeals in court.

1965 On February 14, at about two-thirty in the morning, Malcolm's house is set on fire. One week later, on February 21, Malcolm X is assassinated in the Audubon Ballroom in Harlem. He is thirty-nine years old.

1966 Talmadge Hayer and two other men are convicted of murdering Malcolm X. They are sentenced to life in prison. But questions remain about who was involved in Malcolm's death.